Precious Veyonne Belief

A Mourning Dawn

Cole Wynter

Precious Veyonne Belief

A Mourning Dawn

Cole Wynter

Wynter Knights Publishing
Los Angeles

A WYNTER KNIGHTS PUBLICATION

First Edition

Copyright © 1997 by Cole Wynter

All rights reserved. No part of this publication maybe reproduced, stored in a retrieval system, or transmitted, in any form or by any means, electronic, mechanical, photocopying, recording, or otherwise, without prior written permission from the publisher.

ISBN: 978-0-6151-4822-9

Wynter Knights Publishing
Los Angeles, CA

Dedicated To
My Baby, My Angel
My Love

From
Your Baby, Your Poet
Your Love

I Love You Precious
Forever & Always

"EVER KNOW THAT WHAT YOU FEAR IS WHAT YOU FIND"
- Bush, from the song *Greedy Fly*

"IF YOU MAKE YOURSELF VULNERABLE ON PAPER YOU'LL HAVE NO MORE INSECURITIES"
- Comedian Ray Grant

Table of Contents

A Sandy Haze 1

A Paler Shade of Wicked 28

A Mourning Dawn 37

Chapter One:
A Sandy Haze

"Geometric Progression"

I'm Sorry I Forgot

Frightened
by hazel green eyes
that haunt my sleep
filled with insomnia
as ghostly memories
tease my imagination
with a smile
that launched
a thousand dreams
into an arctic wasteland
that couldn't remember
the last time
the sun rose

Smooches

I used to know a girl
that would kiss me on my lips
nothing special
sometimes mouth open
sometimes not

another used to bite me
not hard
just enough
my lower lip
my tongue
lightly sucking both

this one would moan
just a little
softly and with intention
with a moist warmth
that comforted
my uneasy heart
as her tongue tasted mine

once this girl kissed me
like the sun
wouldn't be back
the next day
one hand massaging
the nape of my neck
the other holding me tight
as her lips caressed mine
and her tongue
twisted and intertwined
with my own
as she tried desperately
to convince it to live with hers

And then there was one
that made me think
there was no one else
that was worth kissing
she would hold me
and touch her lips to mine
like I was the only thing
that had ever mattered
long… slow… deliberate…
she would lick my lips
taste my tongue
and caress my mouth
as she rubbed my back
holding my head
she would steadily
kiss her way around
my face
with tears in her eyes
making my mouth
as jealous as
a stepchild
returning to it in time
flavoring the inside
with strawberry peaches
that hauntingly stalked
every kiss thereafter
finding comfort
in mediocrity
as my lips ache
for something tender
and my tongue
wonders
what your kisses taste like

Shook

Her mouth fluttered
in the darkness
as she read
her voice
speaking
in a tongue
native enough
for my soul
to comprehend
as her words
baked the story
into a luscious cobbler
that tasted peachy tart
and her lips
were close enough to eat

Precious

A baby's laugh
drifts across a summer breeze
into the hearts of a couple
chillin' in the park
under a blue clear sky
wrapped in each others affection
radiating in the smile
of a granddaddy
finding comfort
in his children's children
remembering when his wife
was around to hold him tight
like the friends at the bus stop
each dearly loving the other
too afraid to ask for more
than the price of admission
to a second rate romance
deciding on an evening
of conversations and sunsets

Slippin'

My heart skipped some beats
as I passed her in the hall
and when I noticed her talking
to someone else it started to slip
through my system
luckily my stomach caught it
as I messed around
the other end of the hall
waiting for her conversation to be over
and when it was
I approached
and said my wassups
questioning
whether I could walk with her
so we went through the halls
silence the only thing
keeping us together
my mind decided
(against my will)
to not think
of something interesting
as we stopped at the class
where her friend
would be leaving soon
(somehow I managed to find that out)
and my traitorous brain
made my treacherous mouth
form the question
whose answer I already knew

"How do you feel about me?"
"What do you mean?" she said
"Do you like me at all?"
"As a friend," she said

my heart crumbled to pieces
slid through my stomach
and oozed out my belly button
shattering even more
into a million shards
of red mercury
as it hit the floor

"A friend."
"mm-hm," she said
"OK."

with a face born
from a poker game
never played
I picked all the pieces
I could catch off the floor
with all the dignity
I ever had
told her I would see her later
and made my way
down the hall
searching for the comfort
the truth should have given me

Alms

I wanted to cry
myself to sleep
because all she wanted
was my friendship
even though
I had so much more to offer

Fugitive

Sitting alone in my room
amongst the bills
and magazines
and clothes
staring blankly at the TV
as it flashes
momentary preoccupations
that get recorded
on the back of my brain
like those mix tapes I make
to listen to in my car
as the hollowness
in my big red heart
and the ache
in my empty round belly
cold cocked me
back to my dark corner
just in time to notice
the time I saved in my closet
escaping out the window

Tears

When I was eleven
I shed my last tear
losing a good friend
to an accidental bullet
my mother seeing the Pain
tears flowing freely like a rapid river
silent secret vows
never cry again
years going by
discovering the feeling of a broken heart
being baited by false pretense
and lured in
Heart crumbling to pieces
thankful for self promises
the Pain staying hidden

life devoid of substance

drowning in alcohol
life in
Danger
grades slipping, pressure from counselor/teachers
hating life like a rainy day
fatal blow to the crumbled heart
Papa
great grandfather
friend 'til forever

leaving without saying bye
calling God, asking why
but his phone was off the hook
gathering the pieces of my already broken Heart
burying them in my emotional cemetery

emptiness becoming more empty

still grateful
for tearless eyes
just like now
feeling your fires burning my Heart
back to life like half used charcoal
only to be extinguished
by my resurrected fears
stabbing my soul
with icy daggers of isolation
the pain from your absence
like a broken leg
to the stubbed toe
of your detached presence
my barren soul standing strong
not showing the Pain
still keeping the tears at bay

Showers

Sometimes
I sit in the shower
and let the water
run down my face
and it almost feels
like real tears

Internal Rain

The water came from nowhere
trying to fill an empty place
with cool that washed away
the cleanliness of a righteous heart
tainting it with putrid thoughts
unsoothing an uneased soul
stinging my eye's mind
with acidic truth
that burned cold trails
of insight
through my body
as the rain hit harder
with the thunder whispering
nothing sweet in my ears
and lightening struck the past
flashing it to the present
that the wind twisted
forcing me to cling
to whatever
wasn't stable
as the rain beat me down
while my face
stayed dry

Woe

A blue black sky
hung low under my head
as clouds scraped my face
every time I looked up
hoping the sun
would be back
to kiss away the stain
of a tearless eye

Fate

She said she couldn't breathe
because of the magnitude of my
presence
(me feeling the same about her)
as I caressed her back
she said my hands felt good
to me her back felt good
we both laid breathless
uneasy by the light
which was easily extinguished
still rubbing her back
I touched my lips to hers
and she returned my affection
passion for passion
and I felt my Pain slip away
hoping it would never return
unsettled by the fact no one had
ever done that before
wanting her to keep it away
wondering if another could
we continued to kiss and caress
becoming partly undressed
but never going too far
as my hands memorized her shape
comparing it to another (others)
and my mouth tasted her flesh
as she did mine
moaning my name as I did hers
thinking of another (others) moaning
still telling me how good my hands felt
thinking how good she felt
our bodies pressed together for what
seemed like a college career
my heart aching for this moment to
never end
wondering if she was my equal
laughing to myself at such absurdity
I felt her tremble
(me remembering another (others)
trembling)
once... twice
(damn she was beautiful)

She said she was tired
I wasn't
she had to get up early
I didn't press the issue
she gave me the option
leave or stay
choosing the latter
not wanting her to think
that was all I was there for
wanting her to know I was different
(me not wanting to leave her)
we slept the night through
waking before the sun
we hugged
she didn't want to kiss
mutual morning breath
(me not caring)
knowing another (others) wouldn't care
feeling something different in her touch
still caring... still longing... but...
we talked for a moment
about future plans of our togetherness
already aching to see her again
I left
she closed the door behind me
my Pain came back
and I haven't heard from her since

Wavering

I hesitated
for just a flash
of a red ambulance light
as I shook to dial
anticipating her harmony
for a ring and a half
stumbling to conversate
hearing that thing
in her voice
that didn't want to talk
deciding to call me back
cause I couldn't compare
to another
movie of the week

Pain

Please
take me away
and bless
the life I lost
to the cold
that made me
ache
for the attention
of an
unconcerned
heart

Freedom

Lone bums
in isolated alley corners
that harbor forgotten toys
of children
that play by themselves
in backyards made for families
that don't know how to get along
breaking apart like Voltron
going separate ways
like lonesome lovers
that only want each other
but don't know how to be together
intersecting like merging traffic
with other crumbled hearts
that cling like Saran Wrap
suffocating a soul
with plastic pretensions
that give off toxic fumes
by the burning appetite of freedom
that flows from lips
like diarrhea
that everybody hates
wanting to be mated
to another spirit
so they don't become
like forgotten bums
in alley corners

Love

Slept away to bliss
didn't matter
If it did
leave me wanting
never enough
to make it stop
don't leave
go away
don't go
I left
make me whole
like before
I miss the way
everything makes sense
when you aren't around
all I wanted was the magic
it seemed real
I didn't know it was only for the minute
cause the moment didn't matter

Desolate

You tried
to rip out my Heart
without even
realizing
what you were doing
cracking open
my sternum
and reaching into
the void
only to discover
the remnants
of a heart long ago killed
by someone
just like you
me having buried it
in my mind's backyard
my emotional cemetery
in that plot
right next to its companion
the Love
I can no longer give
their unified epitaph reading:
"Here lies my Heart
and my Love
soulmates for eternity
when one died
the other had no choice
but to follow"

Shelter

Drifting through a desert storm
I met an oasis
that quenched
my dry pasty mouth
brought back my spit
and shaded me
from sand burns
with palmy trees
that gave color to a
monochromatic landscape
as I faded
into a dream
about a tragic soul
and a hopeless heart
searching for the raiders
of a lost love
awaking on a sandy bed
to see the oasis
shimmying into the distance
as I prayed to God
to keep it close

Thirsty

Roaming
through my life's Sahara
I tried
to drown my sorrows
in the waters
of others
but
your sensual pool
had finally quenched
my thirst
and when I needed
another drink
you left me
to fend for myself
as the hot desert sun
beat steadily upon me
searching
for other waters
to ease
my parched throat
but
they are like
salt water
each drink
making me
more needful
of your
fresh water oasis
becoming more thirsty as I drink
drinking to ease my thirst
becoming more thirsty...
as the sun
like a vice
slowly squeezes
the sweat
from my pores

Deluded

I see you all the time
vague Xerox reproductions
connecting like paper clips
deluding myself
with special effects
and camera tricks
for awhile
seeing through similarities
like clear glass
a window shopper
at Macy's
deciding not to purchase
hearing Memorex voices
of you
as I move to the next store
not settling
for cheap copies
from Kinko's

Damn

Sittin' in my room
kicked back
hat pulled low
surrounded by
a soft blue light
sippin' on a Soft and Wet
with a twist of lemon
lamenting with a Prince
that fancies himself
an Artist
about the possibilities
of becoming
your girlfriend

Words

Reaching out with distant eyes
a soul touched mine
swirling and mixing
the whole of two same halves
sharing a smile
with no words between us
just a gap
that crossed the world
caressing my mind
with self defeating thoughts
laid brick after cement
so thin
the words didn't even try
to break through
as I watched those eyes
in the distance
through the concrete
as they grew and changed
remaining the same
while the words still hid
in the back of my throat

Caress

Sparkle

Sifting
through a sensual sand
brown… warm…
sinking quick
into a dusk shade
fleeting past
on a forward journey
left to find
an open day
across the last turnover
of a lunar
mourning
rising
to meet
a sparkling lady
black
as a dreamless sleep
easing the love
of a passionate frost…

Glaze

…in a misty haze
of frosty heat
a second third
came to a sandy wash
to soothe
the yearn
for chocolate syrup
poured
leisurely
fresh… steamy…
under
a honey coated moon
golden slick
with carmel bliss

Sleepy

…exploding like a flowers bloom
over hot gray skies swirling into
a purple sea of "week" power
on a septic boulevard filled with
sleepy beach blue dreams
wrapped up in lonely sandlot
not watching any more games
with no players, on account of rain,
as I rolled over and stayed awake

Relaxed

Holding on to life
ours lips found places
that made us sigh
skin
slick and creamy
gliding our touches
over comforting
curves
pelvis caressing
my desire to erupt
slowly
more urgent
steam filled eyes
that never saw me before
kissing me
with the breath
of a lustful calm
reaching for me
heart jumping
staying on beat
easily
surrounded
awed by the passion
of soft warm strokes
climbing the stairs to bliss
two and three steps at a time
savoring
unmatched joy
as our affection
exploded
on to Heaven's gates
looking up
into an angel's smile

Pieces

Shattered glass
from a reckless vandal
just because
the only reason
Lego houses get broken
by jealous siblings
to see the pain
in their brothers
or sisters eyes
that shed sea turtle tears
over spilled orange juice
that stains the table
still standing strong
after decades of abuse
like a battered wife
taught to believe
she deserves the furious fists
of a boy too weak
to stop himself
too blind to see
his misdirected anger
at a job unfulfilling
like an aquarium
with a leak
that nobody cares enough to fix
a shattered soul
that lies on the floor
in pieces
that don't seem to fit
together
a million piece puzzle
that is only one color
like the sky
on a clear day

Chapter Two:
A Paler Shade of Wicked

"Chaos: Death Against Death"

A Family

BEFORE I KNEW IT SHE WAS PREGNANT
EVEN THOUGH WE DIDN'T PLAN IT
SHE WAS SO CRUSHED SHE COULDN'T FUNCTION
AS SHE DRIFTED THROUGH HER SORROW
WITH SWOLLEN EYES THAT HAD RUN OUT OF TEARS
I WAS SO PROUD
BRAGGING AND BOASTING MY CLAIMS TO FATHERHOOD
BLIND TO HER SUFFERING
THAT KEPT HER AWAKE THROUGHOUT THE NIGHT
AS I SLEPT SOUNDLY
COMFORTED BY THE FACT
THAT THE WOMAN I LOVED WAS HAVING MY CHILD
EVEN THOUGH NEITHER ONE OF US
WAS READY
I TOLD HER I WOULD ALWAYS BE THERE
FOR HER AND OUR BABY
AND SHE HUMORED ME WITH ALL THE TALK
OF A FAMILY LIFE THAT I WANTED TO HEAR
EVEN THOUGH WE WERE YOUNG
I KNEW WE COULD MAKE IT WORK
BUT SHE DIDN'T TELL ME
THAT SHE NEVER WANTED TO HAVE CHILDREN
AND I ONLY FOUND OUT
THE DAY AFTER THE FUNERAL
WHEN THE MAILMAN HANDED ME
THE LAST THING SHE HAD EVER WRITTEN

Danger

I once did some stupid shit
hangin' with my boy
and his boys
(that I didn't know)
wallowing in my own decadence and self-loathing
as I guzzled 40 after 40
until I was overtaken
by a rum and Coke filled with Oblivion
unaware of the conspiracy
(learning the hard way not to drink with strangers)
as my boy's boys' plotted
my boy left outnumbered
so I continued my binge
until one in particular decided that my ass needed kickin'
because I looked like my cousin
(who wasn't my cousin)
my boy trying to get me out the back
me too fucked up to notice
I remember like a fractured dream
stumbling down... leaning...
trying to articulate my incoherence...
outside falling...
looking up at a fuzzy attacker...
I wake up home
under a blanket
on the couch
in my underwear
"How the fuck did I get here?"
dizzy headache
pasty dry mouth
aching body
returning to the scene of ignorance
looking for my hat
amazed looks from those who witnessed my Bacardi blitz
discovering my danger with a detached point of view
by he who thought it would be cool
for me to die
because my tiny forehead scratch
my forgotten humiliation
and not looking like I had been beaten up
was not enough
and for the first time in my life
I knew what it was like for a man to want me dead
more disturbed than fearful
seeing everything in the third person
I deliberated for a time...
eventually left it up to God
and walked without fear
and to this day I am alive and well
while he that would do me harm
is long since dead

Apples

Candy apple cunt
all ripe and pure
let me take a mouthful
to see if U
are as sweet
as your
caramel coated glaze
I want to core
U out
and put U
on my stick
apples and Sin-namon
but not too
quick
to cover U with
milk
lick off the sticky
first
warm and moist
fresh
out the wrapper
and ready to tongue

...Wish I Had Some Ice Cream

I want to taste you
and lick
your tight sin-namon
body
the way a kid
tongues ice cream in a sugar cone
on a 90° day
savoring it
to make it last
the whole summer

Disgusted

Raw red meat
with fat juicy maggots
in her mouth
and the thought
of kissing her
was even
more arousing

Slit

The blood
seemed to drip

...slowly
water torture
Chinese style
I once saw in an old war movie
100 drops to insanity
Charles Manson on LSD
a role model
for Christian youth
crimson trickle

...splashing
softer than
my affectionate wrath
against caramel pools
on to semen stains
slick and white
piled salty on pink satin
lush mortality

...fusing
nuclear cold
with megatons of appetite
unmatched by a million
half starved Ethiopians
in a Martian wasteland
creamy sacrament

...exploding
like tobacco spit
on concrete flesh
in a vacuum abhorred by nature
into a black sky
with bloody rain
hot with Habañero sauce
steamy consecration

...seeping
through a barren grave
filled with the emptiness
of a soul
too hard to sleep
over rotting shit
from a dog with dysentery
consumed by wicked flies
bringing Death
back to life

My Bloody Rose

I picked my rose
bloody
yesterday
to keep it close
watching from the inside
hurt too much
pulling it from the dirt
I cut myself
on a thorn
a large gaping wound
that spilled nitrogen
on the ground
freezing on contact
my rose
began to bleed
gushing warm coagulated clumps
all over me
ruining my fresh new outfit
I wore just for her
stinging my eyes red
I tried to stop the flow
only making it worse
the bush erupting
in silent accusation
doing my best to make it stop
calming the bush
my rose
myself
her blood tasting strawberry sweet
drinking freely
to keep her in my heart
I laid next to her in the cold crimson mud
as she wilted
watching with hollow eyes
as I caressed her soft petals
running fingers over thorns
not quite as pointy
I cradled her in my arms
and kissed
her pollen soaked cheek
returning inside
Kelvin had set the thermostat to ZERO
still wanting her close
I curled up with her in the corner
when the windows frosted over
as I waited for the Devil
'cause all flowers go to Heaven

UNFORGIVEN

HEAVEN HAD NO FURIES
FOR MY VENGEANCE
AS i DROWNED
IN AN ICY POOL OF DEPRAVITY
PROCEEDING DOWN A VICIOUS ROAD
IN A VEHICLE OF REVENGE
RUNNING OVER ANY AND ALL
THAT CROSSED MY LANE
ONE BY TWO… THREE… FOUR…
HOW MANY MORE
TO HIDE THE FRIGID GRAVE
OF A FROZEN HEART
A KID AT THE PLAYGROUND AGAIN
SLEEPWALKING
DREAMING AS A STRANGER
STILL ON THE 666TH HIGHWAY
JUST ENOUGH GAS
TO FINISH
NO MORE LOOT
FOR THE RETURN TRIP
HAUNTED
BY THE MEMORIES
OF THOSE CRUSHED
STILL CRUSHING AS i APPROACHED
THE PLACE
WHERE THE ROAD ENDED
AND HELL HAD NO MORE JOYS
FOR MY SORROW

Chapter Three:
A Mourning Dawn

"The Waker Sleeps"

If

If I touched your hand
would you pull away?
Would you take hold of mine
touch it to your face
and wrap it around your waist?
Would you interlock our fingers
like our souls in a steamy dream
I once had?
Would you not be shy and touch me back
caressing my hands like long lost friends?
Would I restore your faith
and make the world a good place?
Would you touch my face
and hold it close to yours?
Would you make us complete?
Would you let me…
just touch your hand?

Enchanted

My heart ached
more than my muscles
the day after an intense workout
with every glance
feeling a calm
as cool as a tropical breeze
detouring through Phoenix
at the touch of a hand
knowing I was home
when our longing
broke the surface
exploding with tender caresses
long slow kisses
and hugs
that kept the world away
as our affection
gave her
the tears that people get at weddings
and I couldn't remember
the last time I was happy

Reflection

I saw you today
were you thinking of me?
your head was low
preoccupied with a cuticle
or a palm line

was it me you were thinking of?
remembering my fingers tracing
a path over your lobe
through your hair
stopping to rub
that spot
behind your ear
as your head rubs back
my hand getting wet
from your tears
and the tracks
they left behind

were you thinking of my lower lip?
the way it tasted
between your teeth
maybe it was my tongue
you were thinking of
remembering the way
it slowly slid
around your mouth
until it met yours
hugging like
two best friends
that didn't know that
after all these 24 years
they were still in love

I saw you today
thinking of me…

was it just a hang nail?

Transmigration

Haven't we met before?
In another life
at a lush oasis in a vast desert
you wore black
from sole to mind
exposing your eyes
that met mine
cleansing in the sand
praying to the east
disbelieving in polygamy
we rode on my stallion
into the moonrise
and never left each others side

Don't I know you?
from a lifetime ago
we worked in a field
cropping white fluff
in the hot sun
that made us rich
in honey brown complexions
sweating from rooster crow
to cricket chirp
smiling for real
when our eyes
could only see each other

Didn't I meet you?
seven souls ago
before the world knew
people existed on islands
in the middle of the ocean
with white beaches
clear blue water
and balmy summer breezes
all year round
that cooled my body
wet from shark hunting
I watched you
picking mangos
embarrassed when you saw me
as the sun
put a gleam in your eyes
that tore me to you
I gave you a fish
you gave me a fruit
and we held each other
until the sun went down

Don't you remember?
when our souls were young
we didn't know
faces could be pale
in our valley forest
by the lake
collecting skins
to trade for your beads
just to watch
your eyes sparkle
with the intensity
of a clear summer night's sky
filled with millions
of tiny snowflakes
that caressed your face
almost as tenderly as I did
when we would visit each other
holding hands while the moon
danced on the water

Your eyes never change

Empathy

Does he know who you are?
when you dive deep into his eyes
like cliff divers
in Acapulco
searching for the tenderness
of a conch
on the inside of it's shell

Can he see your fractured soul?
the cracked ice
you knew was too thin to skate on
but pure will
kept you from falling in

Does he make you feel like a woman?
when he leaves you
to get hit by the door
on your way in (out)
as you wonder why
he never kisses your cheek
just because...

Does he feel your emptiness?
when you let him in
pretending to be caring
wishing you were somewhere
(someone) else
as he reaches the summit
thinking you both climbed the mountain
while you never left the lodge
curled by the fireplace
with a hot cup of cocoa
sparking your own embers

How does it feel?

We

If I was... you
would you love me?
would you touch myself
like T-Boz
trimming my garden
with the skill of a Japanese monk

If I was... you
would you love me?
would you cleanse myself
in a seaspray bath
shaving & exfoliating
to make me smooth

If I was... you
would you love me?
would you dress myself
in silks and satins
just tight enough
to make me as sexy
as Dorothy Dandridge

If I was... you
would you love me?
would you want myself
to be cared for
like that picture
of Jesus
Michaelangelo painted

If I was... you
would you love me?
would you love myself
enough
to love you

Vision

Imagine
the words that would dance on my lips
and slide across my tongue
if YOUR LIPS touched mine

Imagine
the words that would flow from my lips
like water from a breaking dam
if YOUR TONGUE tasted mine

Imagine
the hands that would laugh and play
speaking in a joyous tone
if YOUR ARMS were around me

Imagine
the hands that would read your face
like a blind man reading braille
if YOUR CHEEK was next to mine

Imagine
the heart that would jump and skip
hopscotching to an aching beat
if YOUR CHEST was close to mine

Imagine
the heart that would open wide
like department store doors the day after Thanksgiving
if YOUR BODY was pressed against mine

Imagine
the soul that would soothe and ease
like sugar honey iced tea on a hot June day
if YOUR VOICE called my name

Imagine
the souls that would swirl and mix
like honey and sweat in the moonlight
if OUR BODIES were whole

TOGETHER

Stellar Cartography

I saw myself in the stars the other night
looking for you in the moon
inch by mile
through the shiny gray dust
combing through the rocks
for that lunar pearl
only to see you over the way
milky fresh
curled up in Andromeda's lap

I saw myself in the stars last night
holding your hands across the sky
strolling through a Saturn rain
bathed in a red glow
from a Jupiter storm
taking comfort
in a comet
my man Halley let me grip
cruising south to watch
an Auroran Dusk

I saw myself in the stars tonight
touching your face over the earth
draped in a blind
Venutian heat
exploring a planet in the heavens
lost in velvet black
smooth as a sweaty solar flare
caressing constellations
into a nebula
of sleepy bliss

Shiver

Does your heart still quiver
when you see me?
when our eyes meet like sweethearts
from high school
that knew they were
the only love
that would last

Does it jump like mine
when you're near me?
having visions
of a cupid
playing a bad joke
as I reminisce
with 112 reasons
to want you close

Does it shake
like a scared dirty bunny
during rabbit season?
when I hold you
in my arms
that fit better
than OJ's
alleged gloves

Does it play hopscotch
or double dutch
when I say your name?
the way mine does
when you tell me
how much
your lips
still love me

What does your heart do
when I look into your eyes?
hoping to catch you
wanting to catch me

Wanting to understand
the mystery

Can you see my heart?

Silence

Did you hear me today?
I was thinking of you
I had a fantasy
that we were friends
walking by Sweetwater Creek
under a silver spotlight
blessed by the moon
we were holding hands
watching the water ripple
from a night owl duck
I was whispering your name

Did you hear me today?
I was remembering your smile
I had a dream
that it was a cinnamon moon
lighting a path
to Heaven's Emerald gates
you were a mahogany angel
dressed in black
holding my hand to show me
who I was

Did you hear me today?
I had a thought
that you were thinking of me
and how my eyes
would smile
when you would see
your heart beating
like hummingbird wings
the first time
we held each other
hoping
we could keep
the world together

Did you hear me?
I was calling you
trying to get your attention
so you wouldn't forget...

You still had my heart

Why

Sometimes late at night
I lie awake
with tear filled eyes
that can't remember how to cry
asking God why he teased me
with your kisses
that took away the Pain

'round Midnight

It was about
'round midnight
when she descended
slowly casting a silhouette
over my ghost
as her shadow covered
the half light
that made me comfortable
taking my heart
in her hands
she made it hollow
enough to care
as she drew me
in her personal space with wings
on my shoulders
like I saw in a story book once
caressing my cheek
with tears
from her face
she wrapped me with feathers
fresh and pure
taking me to the 9th cloud on the right
under a peach moon
downy soft
like my black sweatshirt
right out the dryer
we laid in a cumulus mist
with half open eyes
reading our spirits
to each other
before sleep covered us
in a sandy haze

Musing

"My Baby"

Her voice
tasted sweeter
than any song
the radio had ever played
cradling me in her arms
the down on her shoulders
caressing my face
more relaxed
than a lazy snowfallen
winters night
by the fireplace
I recited a poem
about what happened once
'round Midnight

"My Poet"

Her words
embracing my soul
as her tears
found their way
to my heart
drowning in a happy sorrow
like parents
that lose their children
to colleges out of state
I kissed her luscious woes
as her feathers
lifted us to the stars
holding for an eternity
that lasted half a minute
she let me drift
into space
with a yearn in her eyes
that children get
when they see that one toy
they really want for Christmas

"Goodnight Love"

Her phrase
grabbed my spirit
slowing my re-entry
as the clouds
swallowed me
like raisins sinking
into gray maple oatmeal
she faded into the sky
consumed by condensation
my eyes opened
to a dark room under my covers
and her voice
still echoed in my ghost

'round Noon

It was about
'round noon
when I awoke
on my cloudy bed
wrapped in her wings
she in mine
reading her soul
imprinted on her face
the way the state seal is
on my driver's license
a new born summers night
was not as beautiful
caressing her face
where the tears had been
her eyes spoke
soft and tender
as heaven opened
with her smile
she gave me a kiss
that people give
when they don't
want to say goodbye
more graceful than a swan
she spread her feathers
wide as the Pacific
drifting into the sky
the sun haloed behind her
she held me tighter
than a tourniquet
with her stare
the down from my shoulders
surrounded my heart
and they followed
as she ascended
toward a lunar mourning
leaving me on the 9th overcast
on the right
with no way
to get back to earth

Winded

I looked without breath
the way people do
when they know a bomb
is going to explode in a movie
draped in peach
she stood
a shapely smooth brown
long enough for my mind
to show me a country
undiscovered
where we held hands
speaking with my eyes
she smiled
and stared with eyes
that opened my spirit
flipping through the pages
she skipped the guest list
and put her HANCOCK
on my heart
under permanent resident
showing me her autograph
I wrote mine in her book
as we embraced
with a hope
that would have awakened the dead
we lamented for our dream
laying it down to sleep
she closed my eyes
caressing my dimple
with her lips
she left with my book
and a longing
in our eyes

I Was Sitting By The Bed One Day

I watched her face
as she laid in my arms
more relaxed
than the cooling
afterglow embers
of a night
spent loving someone
you wished was someone else
I kissed
her closed right eye
on the left by the bridge
watching her lips
make a smile
so precious
that I remembered
a sandy brown puppy
my mother wouldn't get me
that sat with big eyes
by an open window
the water swelled
under her lids
and slid down her face
like my orange drink
at McDonald's when they fill it too much
I traced the wet trails
into tiny hearts over her freckles
as her eyes
brown and dark
told me a story about a dolphin
that met a wolf
walking through a pasture
and taught it how to swim
in sweet water
feeling like a father
that's not used to holding babies
while he cradles his first newborn
as she snuggled a little closer
my roommate's cat does that
when he thinks you're not paying
attention
placing her head
on my chest
she leaned up to hug my mouth
the way you do when you missed
someone
more than you could ever tell them
her lips feeling smoother
than my head
wiped clean from shaving magic
we held each other
with the conviction of ice
embracing my windshield
after a winter storm at the beginning of
spring
until a mourning breeze
blew my cobwebs
across the carpet
where they clumped
cold phlegm on a rocky field
just before the last
fragment of my spirit
that felt like summer
in Jamaica
swooped it up
with the fire of a hawk
and followed a silver path
to whereever she was at

www.ingramcontent.com/pod-product-compliance
Lightning Source LLC
Chambersburg PA
CBHW051717040426
42446CB00008B/931